T0160893

CAT WHISKERS

PIE International

15

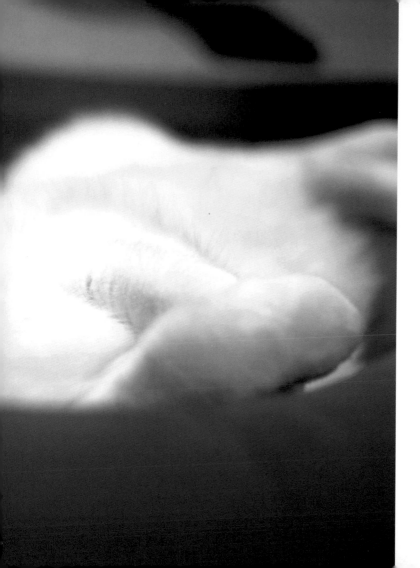

Cat's Mouth Trivia ω

Here are some detailed explanations of a typical cat's muzzle, including the plump "whisker pads" (ω) that define them as cats!

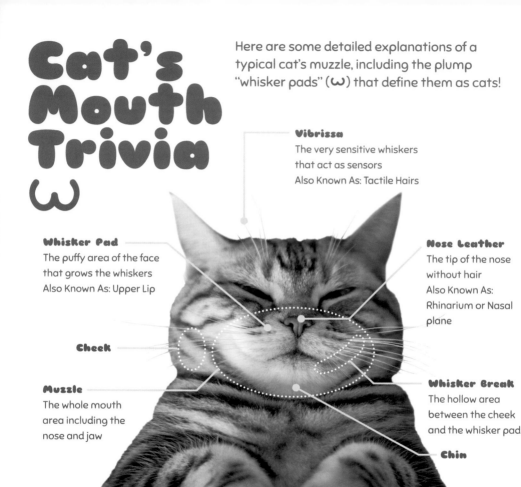

Vibrissa
The very sensitive whiskers that act as sensors
Also Known As: Tactile Hairs

Whisker Pad
The puffy area of the face that grows the whiskers
Also Known As: Upper Lip

Nose Leather
The tip of the nose without hair
Also Known As: Rhinarium or Nasal plane

Cheek

Muzzle
The whole mouth area including the nose and jaw

Whisker Break
The hollow area between the cheek and the whisker pad

Chin

Cat's whiskers

A cat has several types of whiskers around his or her mouth. Each of them plays an important role. You can learn what mood your cats are in just from their movement.

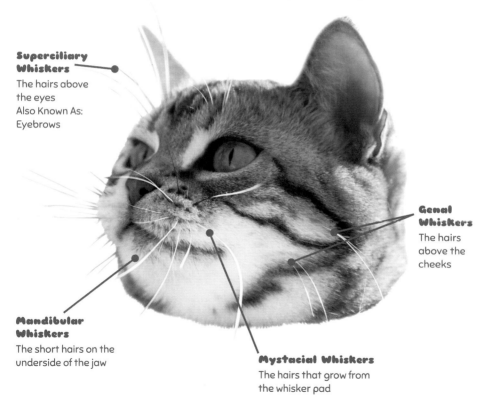

Superciliary Whiskers
The hairs above the eyes
Also Known As: Eyebrows

Genal Whiskers
The hairs above the cheeks

Mandibular Whiskers
The short hairs on the underside of the jaw

Mystacial Whiskers
The hairs that grow from the whisker pad

cat profiles ①

Mari
Inaho

Scottish fold | White bicolor | ♂ |
Osaka
🐾 Inaho_cat
Cover, p6, 7, 24, 25, 39

Mai
Coto

Mixed bobtail | White | ♀ | Tokyo
🐾 maihimemoco
🐾 ameblo.jp/maimocoto
p2, 46, 74

Mai
Moco

Mixed | Brown tabby | ♀ | Tokyo
🐾 maihimemoco
🐾 ameblo.jp/maimocoto
p75

sanchelove
Tsukune

American Shorthair | Brown Tabby |
♀ | Kanagawa
🐾 sanchelove
p2

sanchelove
Tabatha

Scottish fold | Silver | ♀ |
Kanagawa
🐾 sanchelove
p58

sanchelove
Polon

Scottish fold | Calico | ♀ |
Kanagawa
🐾 sanchelove
p70

myacco
Tsuru

Mixed | Mackerel tabby | ♀ | Tokyo
🐾 tsuru.nyan
p2, 48, 49, 50, 51

Pyonko
PONTA

Mixed | Brown & white | ♂ | Osaka
🐾 neconecori
p2, 15

sachio
Azuki

Mixed | Calico | ♀ | Tokyo
🐾 love626gram
p3

Owner's name
Cat's name

Breed | Color | Sex | Location
🐾 Twitter ID
🐾 Instagram ID
🐾 URL
Appeared in pages

mizuha
Pokke

Scottish fold | White & beige | ♂ |
Kanagawa 🐾 pookke 🐾 pookkeboy
🐾 blog.pokkeboy.com/
p4, 5, 28, 47

ramustagram
Ramune

American Shorthair | Silver tabby |
♀ | Kanagawa
🐾 ramustagram
p8, 9, 41, 44, 45, 66, 67

Sumie
Tetsuro

Munchkin | Brown tabby & white |
♂ | Tokyo
🐾 goma_tetsuro
p10, 11, 37

Riepoyonn
Canele

Brown & white | ♂ | Kanagawa
🐾 SoraAmeCane 🐾 Riepoyonn
🐾 ameblo.jp/amecanesora
p12, 13, 26, 34, 35, 55

Riepoyonn
Amelie

Calico | ♀ | Kanagawa
🐾 SoraAmeCane 🐾 Riepoyonn
🐾 ameblo.jp/amecanesora
p12, 13, 27, 34, 35

Riepoyonn
Sora

Black & white | ♂ | Kanagawa
🐾 SoraAmeCane 🐾 Riepoyonn
🐾 ameblo.jp/amecanesora
p15, 62, 78

Rina Takei
PIMMS

Selkirk rex | Orange tabby | ♂ |
London
🐾 rinaguinness 🐾 rina_takei
🐾 ameblo.jp/rina-takei/
p14, 38

Rina Takei
GUINNESS

Domestic shorthair | Black | ♂ |
London
🐾 rinaguinness 🐾 rina_takei
🐾 ameblo.jp/rina-takei/
p16, 17, 65

Makoto
Yuzu

Munchkin | Red tabby & white | ♂ |
Tochigi 🐾🐾 yuzuyuzu_nyan_e
🐾 ameblo.jp/yuzuyuzu-nyan-e/
p15, 68, 69

cat profiles ❷

Tomomi
Hana

Chinchilla | Silver | ♀ | Tokyo
🐾 hanachan_cat
🐾 hanachan.official
p15, 56, 57

JOE
Ura

Scottish fold | White | ♀ | Tokyo
🐾 urabanashi813
🐾 urabanashi813.blog.fc2.com
p18, 19, 32, 33

Suzupon
Ponta

Mixed | Brown & white | ♂
🐾 suzu_pon
p20, 21

ami____5
Coco

Scottish fold | Blue patched
tabby & white | ♀ | Tokyo
🐾 ami____5
p22, 30, 31, 43

ami____5
Moff

British shorthair | Cream tabby | ♂ |
Tokyo
🐾 ami____5
p40, 42, 43

mochikosans
Mochi

Scottish fold | Red tabby | ♂ |
Osaka
🐾 mochikosans
p23, 36, 60, 61

shirukotan
Shiruko

Ragdoll | Blue lynx point mitted |
♀ | Tokyo
🐾 shirukotan
p52, 53, 82

Chiyomame
Mamechiyo

Scottish fold | Blue tabby & white |
♂ | Hokkaido
🐾 chiyomame9cats 🐾 chiyo.mame
🐾 ameblo.jp/chiyomame-9cats/
p54, 81

Chiyomame
Toro

Scottish fold | Silver mackerel
tabby | ♀ | Hokkaido
🐾 chiyomame9cats 🐾 chiyo.mame
🐾 ameblo.jp/chiyomame-9cats/
p64

Chiyomame
Yuzu

Scottish fold | black & white bicolor | ♀ | Hokkaido
🐾 chiyomame9cats 🐾 chiyo.mame
🐾 ameblo.jp/chiyomame-9cats/
p79, 80

Chiyomame
Mikan

Scottish fold | calico | ♀ | Hokkaido
🐾 chiyomame9cats 🐾 chiyo.mame
🐾 ameblo.jp/chiyomame-9cats/
p81

rei_nyanz
Rei

Mixed | Brown & white | ♀ | Tokyo
🐾 rei_nyanz
🐾 peco-japan.com/70037
p72, 73

Myako
Souta

Ragamuffin | Blue tabby | ♂ | Osaka
🐾 🐾 vvviopw
p59

Myako
Kinta

Scottish fold | Cream tabby | ♂ | Osaka
🐾 🐾 vvviopw
p77

tiaichima
Nabby

Scottish fold | Gray | ♀ | Aomori
🐾 tiaichima
p76

IchiTaru
Taruto

Mixed | White & brown bicolor | ♂ | Tokyo
🐾 chatoranekogen
🐾 ameblo.jp/ichitaru22
p63, 71

IchiTaru
Ichigo

Mixed | Red tabby & white | ♀ | Tokyo
🐾 chatoranekogen
🐾 ameblo.jp/ichitaru22
p83

CAT WHISKERS

Editor   Yuka Tsutsui (PIE International)
Art direction   Daisuke Matsumura (PIE Graphics)

Translator   Akiko Tominaga
Typesetting and cover design   Andrew Pothecary (itsumo music)
Production   Aki Ueda (Pont Cerise)

Originally published in Japanese in 2018 by PIE International Inc.
English edition: first published in 2019 by PIE International Inc.

PIE International Inc.
2-32-4 Minami-Otsuka, Toshima-ku, Tokyo 170-0005 JAPAN
international@pie.co.jp
www.pie.co.jp/english

ISBN: 978-4-7562-5222-7

10 9 8 7 6 5 4 3 2 1

Printed in China